SIMPLE TECHNOLOGY

PULLEYS

Liz Lennon and Ellie O'Shea

WINDMILL BOOKS™

Published in 2026 by Windmill Books,
an Imprint of Rosen Publishing
2544 Clinton St.
Buffalo, NY 14224

First published in Great Britain in 2023 by Wayland

Editor: Sarah Peutrill
Designer: Lisa Peacock
Science consultant: Peter Riley

Cataloging-in-Publication Data
Names: Lennon, Liz, author. | O'Shea, Ellie, illustrator.
Title: Pulleys / by Liz Lennon, illustrated by Ellie O'Shea.
Description: Buffalo, NY : Windmill Books, 2026. | Series: Simple technology | Includes glossary and index.
Identifiers: ISBN 9781725397071 (pbk.) | ISBN 9781725397088 (library bound) | ISBN 9781725397095 (ebook)
Subjects: LCSH: Pulleys--Juvenile literature.
Classification: LCC TJ1103.L46 2026 | DDC 621.8'11--dc23

Printed in China

CPSIA Compliance Information: Batch #QW26WM
For Further Information contact Rosen Publishing at 1-800-237-9932

CONTENTS

WHAT IS A PULLEY?

Have you ever seen anyone raising a flag up a flagpole? They pull down on the rope and the flag is raised. They are using a pulley.

A pulley is a simple machine with a rope that goes over a wheel. It is used to lift or move objects, called the load.

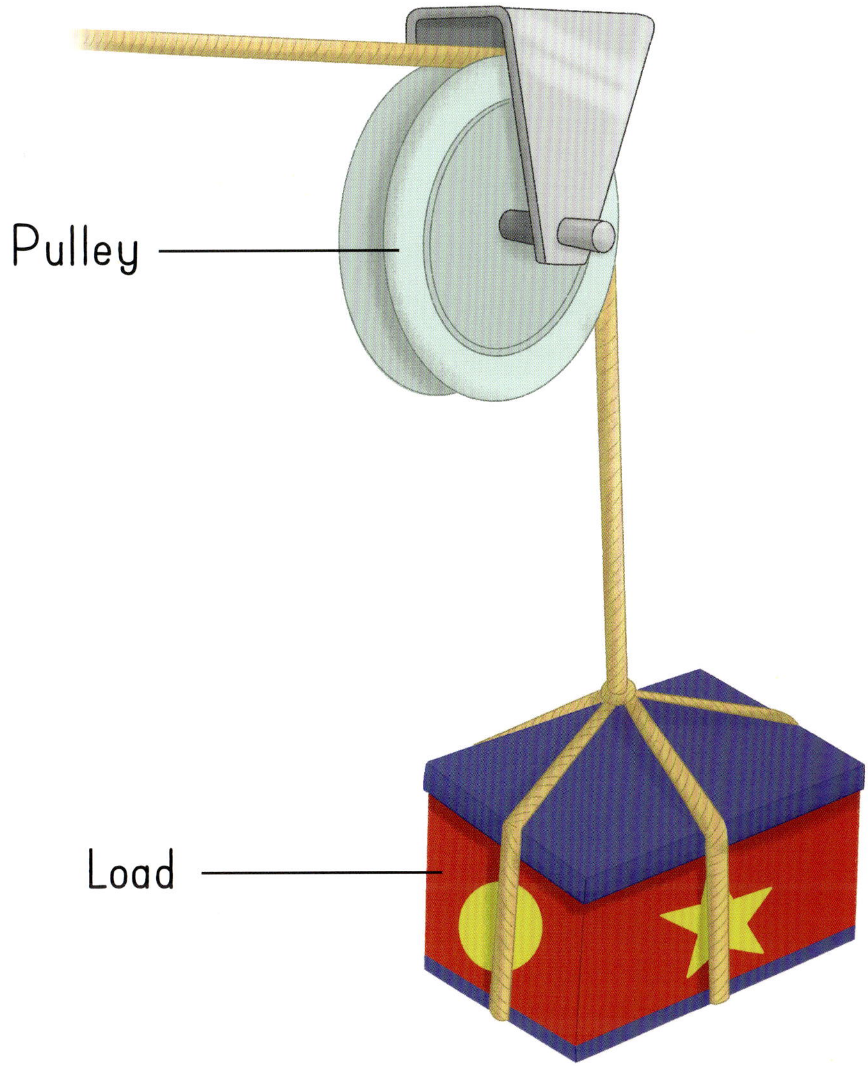

SIMPLE MACHINES

A force is a push or a pull that makes something move. A machine is anything that helps us by transferring a force to where it is needed. A pulley is one type of simple machine.

Pulley

Screw

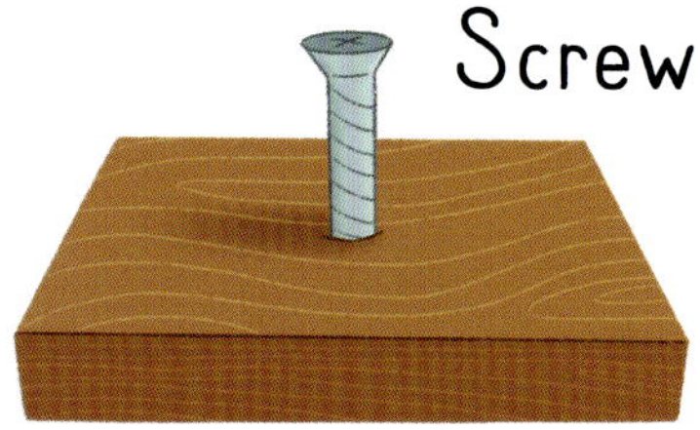

Wedge

Here are some other simple machines.

Lever

Wheel and axle

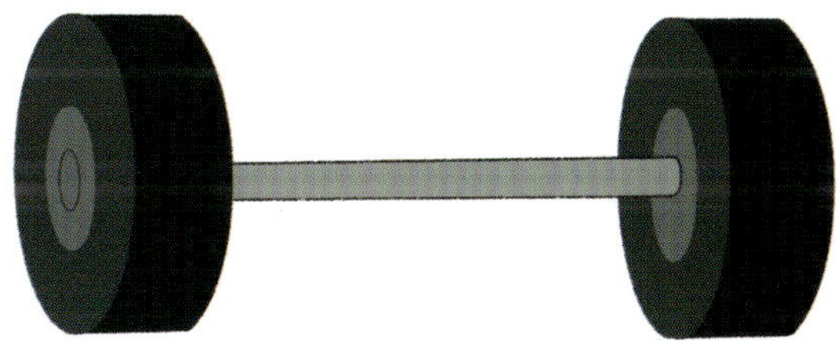

Incline

CHANGING DIRECTION

A pulley allows a small force to be applied over a long distance.

A rope moves around the wheel of a pulley to change the direction of a force. It's easy to move a bucket **up** out of a well, while pulling **down** on a rope.

A SIMPLE PULLEY

Harry has made a simple pulley.
He has tied one end of a piece of
string to a shoe. This is the load.

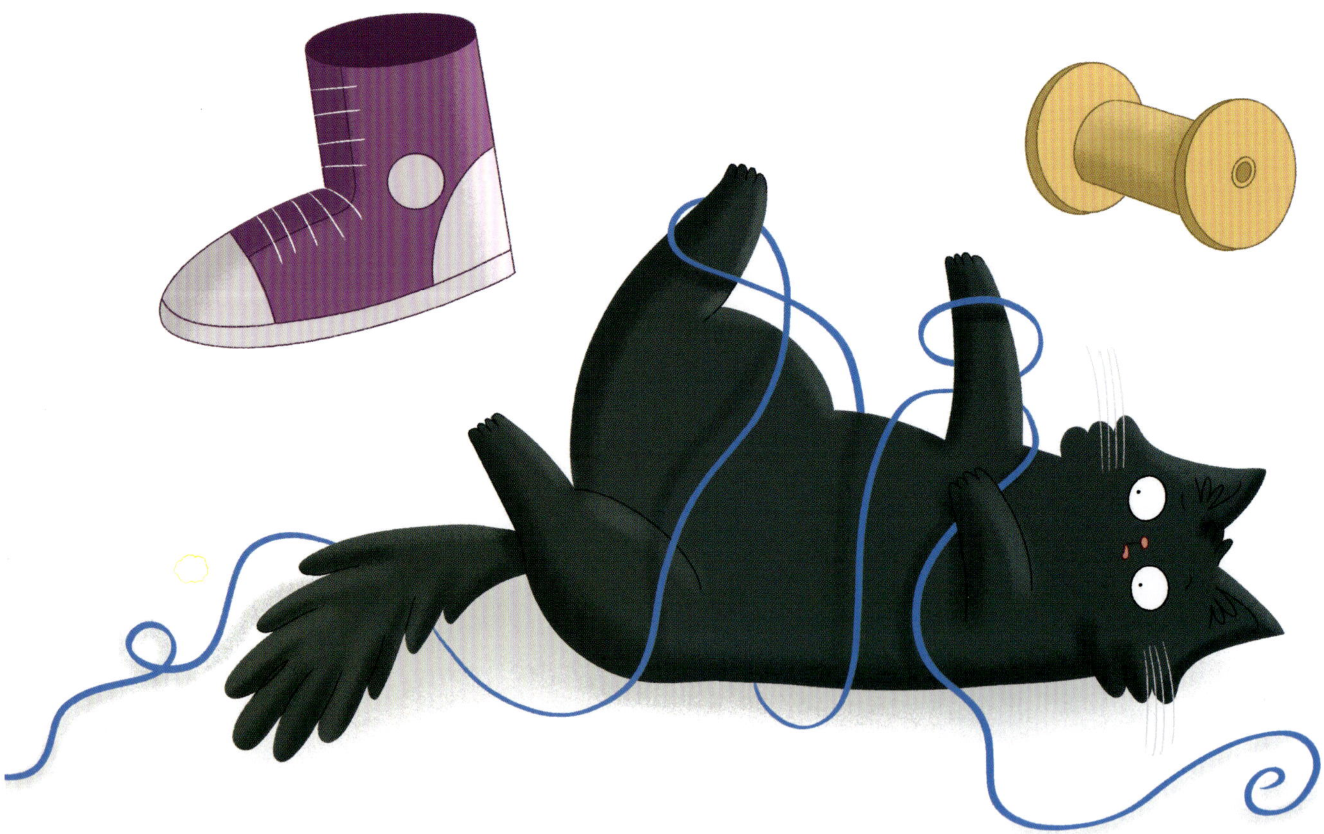

He has looped the string around a cotton reel. Which way will the shoe move when he pulls down on the string?

ON THE BUILDING SITE

There are lots of uses for pulleys. This builder wants to lift a bucket of cement to the person working above.

Using the pulley is much easier than going up the ladder with the bucket.

CLEANING WINDOWS

Tall skyscrapers need to have clean windows.

These window cleaners are being pulled up and down in a platform attached to pulleys.

The pulleys are far above the platform, attached to the top of the building.

ON A BOAT

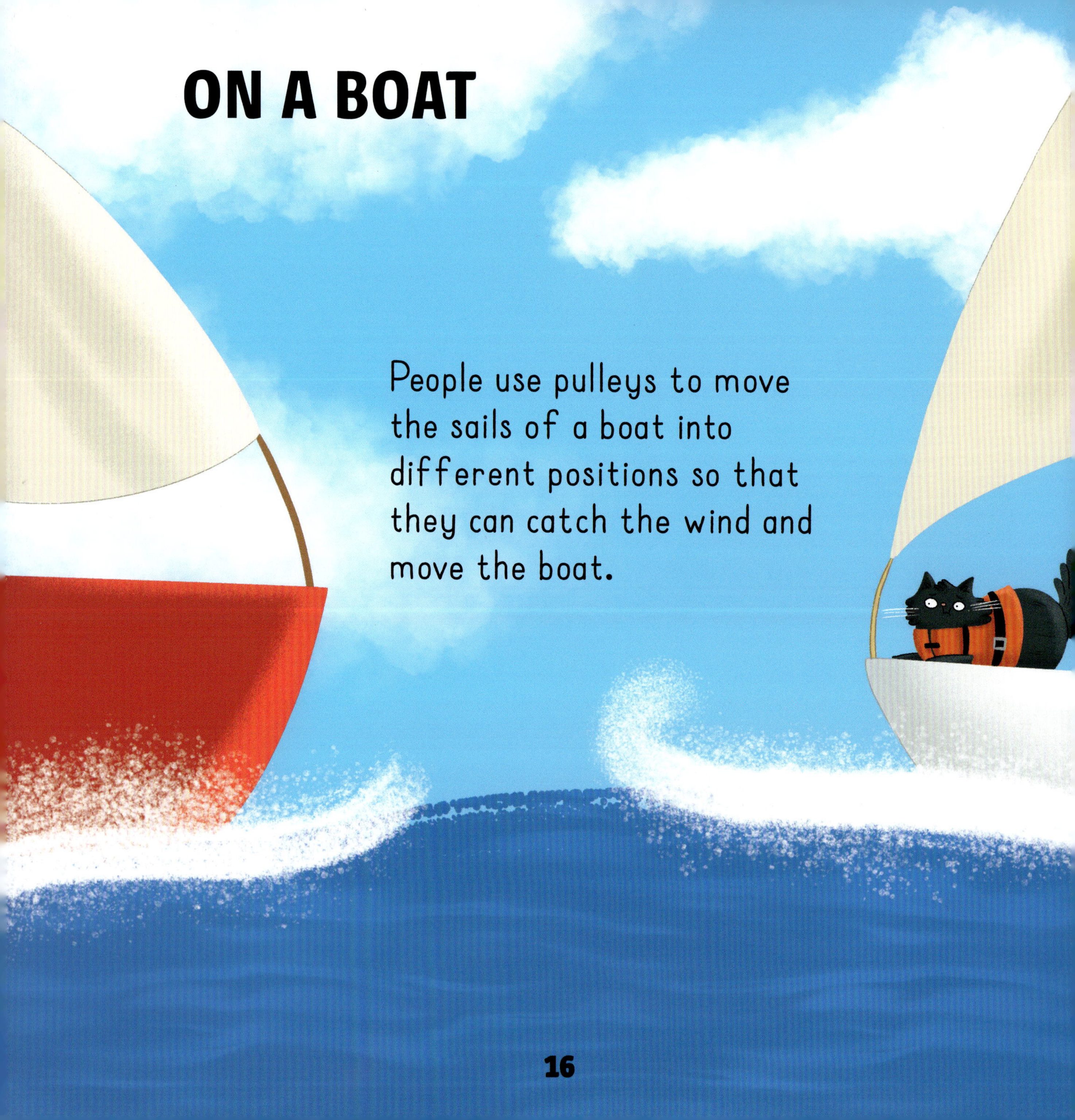

People use pulleys to move the sails of a boat into different positions so that they can catch the wind and move the boat.

Sail
Pulley
Pulley

AT THE GYM

The weights on these exercise machines are moved by groups of pulleys.

Can you find the pulleys in the picture?

IN AN ELEVATOR

Elevators are found in buildings with lots of floors. They are important for people who can't use stairs. Many elevators have steel ropes that raise and lower the car with pulleys.

The car is the part of the elevator you stand in when you go up and down.

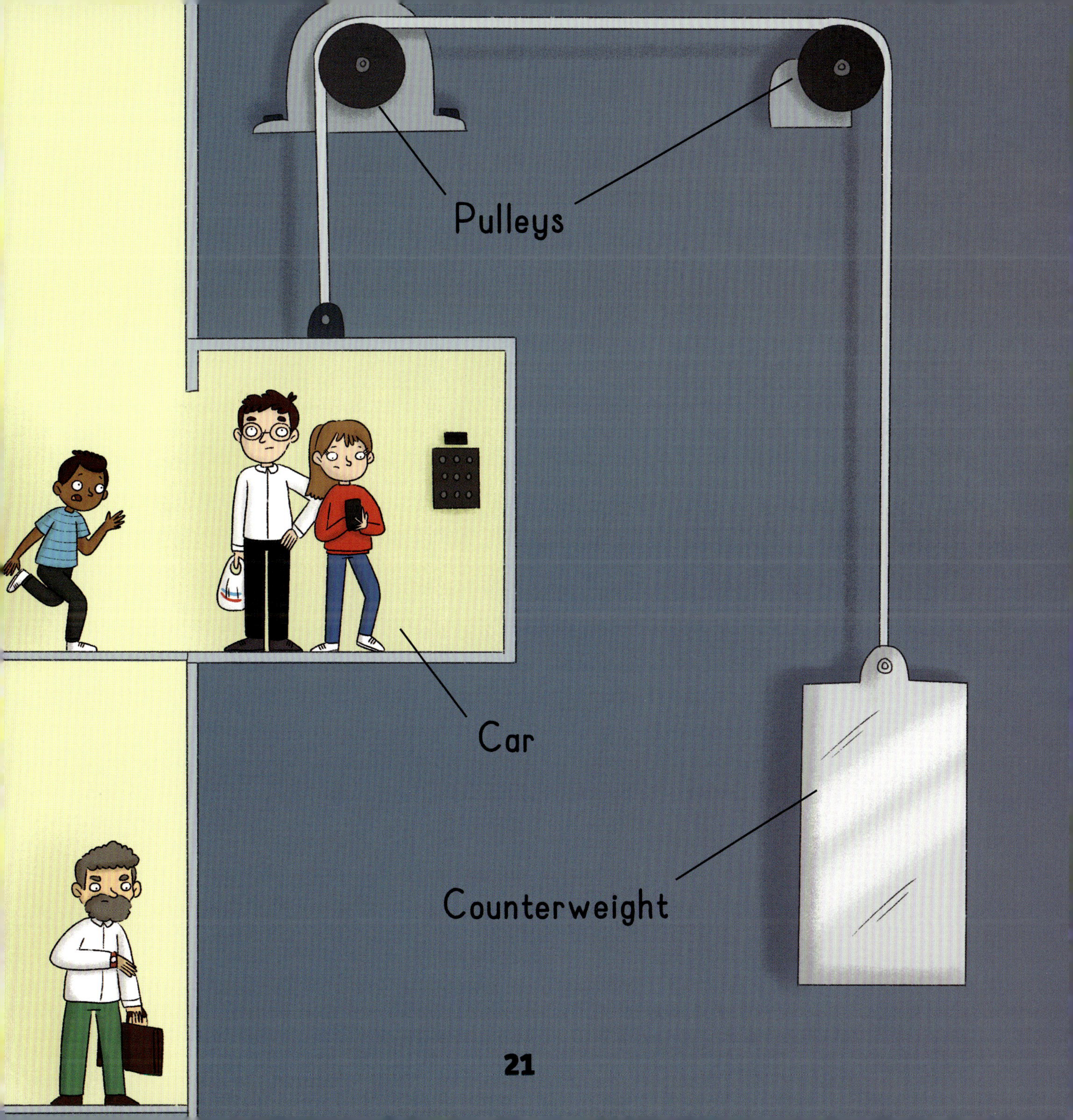
Pulleys
Car
Counterweight

HEAVY LOADS

To lift something heavy, a number of pulleys can be used to make the work easier. The more pulleys you use, the greater the distance you need to pull the rope to lift the load.

Cable cars are very heavy and groups of pulleys help to move them along.

PULLEYS IN A COMPLEX MACHINE

Look at these cranes! Cranes have different parts and use powerful winding machines and pulleys to lift very heavy loads.

FRICTION

When two surfaces touch, there is a force of friction between them. You can feel it pushing against you if you gently push a book on a table.

Push harder and the book slides along because the friction is weaker now. If you stop pushing, the full force of friction returns and the book stops too.

PULLEYS AND FRICTION

Emma has put a rope over a tree branch and attached a bucket to one end. When she pulls the rope, the friction between the rope and branch make it hard to raise the load.

Now Emma has attached a pulley. When she pulls the rope, the friction between the rope and the wheel pulls the wheel around and makes it easier to raise the load.

Pulleys are very useful simple machines for lots of reasons!

GLOSSARY

Here are the key words we explored in this book. Try covering the meanings to see if you can remember them yourself. Were you right?

Axle a rod that two wheels turn on.

Counterweight something that helps to balance some machines.

Force a push or a pull.

Friction a force that occurs when an object rubs against a surface.

Incline a surface where one end is higher than the other.

Lever a machine that reduces the amount of force needed to move an object or lift a load.

Load this is the part that the pulley

moves, such as the shoe and the flag in the pictures.

Machine anything that helps us by taking a force and transferring it to where it is needed.

Muscles the parts of your body that, with your bones, help you to move.

Pulley a simple machine with a rope that goes over a wheel.

Screw a nail-shaped piece of metal with a winding ridge, which is used for holding pieces together.

Squeeze pushing things together.

Weight the heaviness of a person or thing.

Wedge a piece of wood or metal that has one thick end and a thin edge. A wedge is driven between two objects or parts of an object to secure or separate them.

Wheel a circular frame that turns on an axle.

INDEX